DREAMS
and
DISCOVERIES

A STORYBOOK POEM

DANNY WARREN

Printed in the United States of America.

Library of Congress Control Number: 2022939665

ISBN   Paperback   978-1-68536-614-8
              eBook   978-1-68536-615-5

Westwood Books Publishing LLC
Atlanta Financial Center
3343 Peachtree Rd NE Ste 145-725
Atlanta, GA 30326

www.westwoodbookspublishing.com

Dreams and discoveries, now it begins:
The sweetness of death and the silence of sin:
Do you still see me and are you still here,
Ruing the wastage of mistier years?

Time with its parodied pleasantry song
Teases each moment as though it was one
With universe elements need to perceive:
Chastening paradox, prism of greed.

Talk to me when I sleep; tell me it's so;
All you perceive in the world that you know:
Treasures of consequence, yours to enjoy:
Needs of a greedy soul, eyes of a boy.

Care for the past that its timeless embrace
Lets time set its stall in some happier place.

1

I emerge eventually into the subliminal intrusion that is the initial requirement in any dream fantasy, investing itself into my consciousness and easing me relentlessly into a newer awareness of a peculiar perspective that does not signal anything to me of any real comfort or any real promise of elevated contentment either. I am aware that this is an awakening from what has been the long sleep that has been so much the extension of a more prolonged kind of dream time: I am emerging finally into what appears to me to be a rigorous new metamorphosis that is all of my old perceptions and all of my old engagements, purposed by the extension of countless pleading voices, all involved with their own expressions of a similar acquiescence: They are all of the appreciations that are so much akin to the emergence from a deep and enervating sleep into a substantially different paranormal submission of elevated ecstasy: I am engaged with a world that is the travail of so many other relentless clamours, all persisting as issues that I continue to perceive of as being the extension of old songs and even older whispers, continuing to persist as perpetuating promises in this apparently inconsistent eternity. I see this new universe as a satisfactorily replete entity with all of the outpourings of thanksgiving and recrimination, persisting as elemental succours and the abiding promises of a newer and more exciting future. Within this most unsettling of realisations, I am aware that I have once more become invested with a markedly different space and a markedly different state of mind that is an altogether alternative option than any of the ones that I recall having occupied in any of my other previous memory moments: This whole transition experience appears to me to be not too substantially different from any of the ones that I have enjoyed from any of my other recently perceptible pasts: So I must content myself with the continually abiding assumption that I could yet be the only person in this peculiarity that has ever been presented with such an alluringly cynical moment of space and time: It seems to me that this is all of the singularity remnants of a substantially varied circumstance, not too different in fact, from any of the other places and any of the other times that I might once have known from other more endearingly related memory moments; rather more an alluringly alien kind of concept than any of the others that I have comfortably coped with, certainly in terms of all of the new impressions that are even now insinuating themselves into this tentative requirement that is an amicably secure and sensitive assimilation, required of all of these newer and more obligingly inspiratory moments: The immediate impression that I am becoming increasingly aware of in this place is the overwhelming sense of its imperial permanence: I seem as it were, to be drifting in what appears to me to be an interminable expanse of apparently permanent, but still vaguely majestic vacuum paralysis that seems not to have any perceptible extremities that I have been able to perceive of, nor any apparent indications of what the true purpose of this new engagement might actually mean to me either: I perceive the breadth of these limitations, blessed as I have been with a suitably defined perception of all of these apparently copious surroundings: I sense that I have been cast adrift for my sins in what appears to me to be an indolent morass of questionably ephemeral inconsistency that is a readily more amicable and engaging promise of an abiding morality with all of its apparently wishful indifferences, appearing to me to be the meandering uncertainty of so many other limitlessly ephemeral messages, all hastening towards conditions that appear to maintain as unfamiliarly exclusive intrusions into my own inhibited situation: These rarefied parodies of ultra existence are the consequences of so many other engagingly ulterior suggestions, all persisting as the promises of perpetually insistent questions that seem likely to engage me as I proceed through this new future: Readily do these secrecies call out to me as wayward perceptions with which I must learn to live, even though they are all concealed within the surreptitious guises of so many other latent memories that I have always depended on as the lingering inconsistencies that have remained such a large part of this so addled past, for all of my personal assertions and all of the continuing benefits that still maintain as present day mental stabilities: Now they persist only as the conflicts of a mind that is messaging all of the doubts that have been attempting to reform these restrictive constructs, trying continually to impede me as I struggle with all of the questions that still continue to torment me as the elegies of a history that still maintains, even within this new permanence, encased for such a long time in a mirage of ever depleting memory. These chastening demands on my old sensibilities are like a thief that traipses through the limpid night of nocturnal uncertainty, pervading this nervous consciousness and attempting to waylay these trappings of new born visions of which I presently have little or no knowledge, either because of their similarity to previous events or because of any of the real suspicions that still persist, of their true identity. My eyes are now opened to this brave new world that I am beginning to perceive myself as being a part of, yet still see and feel as though it actually has little of real substance that holds anything of purpose for me in this irresolute inconsistency that still maintains as abidingly moral function in this place: With the sights and the sounds that I have previously grown up to be so comfortable with, already beginning to be strangely foreign to me to me, the vestiges of all of this unrequited desperation and longing persists as the remnant of a sadly desiccated past and an uncertainty that still continues to hinder me in this present; so rapturous is this confusion of contradictions with which I have become so ingratiated at this time: I still perceive what is, in its finality, the intensity that is this new perfection of vision and perception, as restrained as this poor presentation will allow it to be. I see only doubt and desperation existing as the lingering essence of this metaphysical incarceration, harbouring the austerity of an awful infinity and the beauty of a congenial spirituality, the like of which has ingratiated its magnificence and its calm into the paled new perception that has become the fruit of this poor soul's hopeful continuation, enabling it always to engage with all of its more sterilizing comforts: It is this balm that is the benevolence of this apparently bizarre emptiness and solitude that is the gift that I must learn to accept, knowing that it might not always be the prize that I might be permitted to retain and enjoy in the vast experience that is this sanctified edifice, free still to engage with for as long as I am permitted to do: So I must substitute my amenable involvement in this inarticulately barren expanse of intangible mayhem for a previous lifetime that seems not to offer much of either identity or familiarity in its construct that I am able readily to relate to in my own mind and also within the perceived limits of this more permanent and unfamiliarly indistinguishable structure.

2

All that I can reasonably continue to do at this time is to dwell on this abiding relic of a past that I do not now perceive of as having any direct consequence or purpose as I continue to adapt to the increasingly differing circumstances of this new and engaging existence, carrying with it so many of the lingering intangibles that I have now become so intrinsically implicated with. The doubtful perceptions of time in this place do not allow me the luxury of understandings that might enable me to relate more readily to the physical restrictions that still play their part in all of the heady processes that govern relationships between this curiously insistent tide of restrictive old memories and the more recent introduction to a life that operates within an entirely different set of circumstances to those with which I have since become more conscious and also more familiar. Recurring messages seem always to be the same whenever I am confronted with the more demanding and emotional moments that constitute my involvement in this journey. With the passage of this new moment that I am now experiencing, it is reasonable to suppose that I might soon be able to identify more readily with some of these memories of my past, simply as a necessary function in areas in which I still nurse hopes of achieving some future promotion in this lifetime, whatever that might eventually mean to me. One significant element of this requirement is the need to secure some semblance of purpose in whatever existence it is that I am now established, still perceiving this whole ethereal experience to be an object lesson in the necessary requirement that is this personal attempt at possibly ephemeral progression that I might eventually be able to relate to in the differing circumstances in which I now find myself.

3

The ponderous impediments that are the most persistently active burden of this recurring memory condition are the devious progenitors that continue to persevere as remnants of old but still jealously guarded implanted regrets: They continue to survive as latent or even treasured recollections, the dregs of an anciently surplus psychological baggage, clinging to an initial focal point of reference and marking the moment when they might reasonably suppose to have arrived, armed only with the tenacity of an unrequited avarice: It is feasible that the retention of memories relating to previous existences still remain a feature of all of the lives of all of the souls that have resided here, to a greater or lesser degree: Regrettably, these negative conditions also maintain with a familar but rabid determination, if only to sustain those lingering impressions of anger and malevolence: The persistence of these feelings of deep seated anger are often exacerbated as organised and orchestrated statements of belligerence that succeed only in alienating the sources of those miseries from the remainder of the multitudes that consist of all of those other entities, all similarly engaged with their own personal ambitions and all with their own personal existences; the recurring essences of those same eclectic dreams and pursuits: The hopes that they all insist on, of maintaining needs that might enable them to finally express that anger, either by a wilful and misdirected determination or by any of the other forms of expression that are popularly employed, as mindlessly relentless acrimony, render these intentions both pernicious and dangerous when they are directed against persons that they still insist in believing are the same instigators of that resentment in the first place: The more extreme manifestations of this misguided intolerance often involve them in numerous mindless expressions of an uncontrollable rage that can often be so intense as to cause them to impose those same negative influences within their own spaces where confrontations of this kind have no place, or even in the different ones that pertain in other areas as well: The tragic consequences of these interventions compel them all to seek for a rather more stable and harmonious location for their own avaricious needs, until a time does arrive that will finally enable them to transfer to a different place which they might then conceive of as being more comfortably and congenially acceptable to themselves: They might then suppose that all of the old regressions that had always sustained them throughout the abusive employment of those distractedly misspent lives might then be discharged as the emotional impediments that had always sustained them, with the damning dispensations and the persistent residues of malice and avarice that had been attached to them, discharged at the same time as well: The consequences of any damage that might have been inherited and transferred as a result of all of those actions might not then be so readily perpetuated in any of the interminable futures with which they might subsequently become involved.

4

The essentials of this spacial conundrum are, I have realised, the more reasonable of these speculative antithesis' of all of the physical conditions that I have always depended on up to and including this particular moment in time, for my own future survival and for my own future comfort as well, particularly with what I have always envisaged, in the past as the extenuation of a previous life condition and the one with which I am already beginning to come to terms: As I am learning to cope with this issue in as amenable a fashion as it is possible for me to do, I have discovered that I might even be better able to achieve considerably improved levels of an ulterior degree of perception that might perhaps stand me in a better stead as I ease my exploratory passage throughout the insidious tracts that maintain as perspective within this convoluted journey: I have even discovered that deriving a moot satisfaction from these indistinct implications that have survived as the remnants of past histories, were not the necessary requirement that I had believed that they might have been for the acquisition of any of the new assimilations that I had once believed to be absolute necessities when related to the requirements of those earlier time lines: The establishment of a successful integration into the workings of this new life style barely enable me even to assert stipulations that might prove to be an adequate survival ethos in the first place, so that future developments and progress might even enable me to become more secure in the end: I might then be able, more comfortably to cope with the physical limitations that these inhibitions have already imposed on the activities of this intentionally liberated spirit.

5

Whispers are the companionships that convey their subliminal messages in this benignly ephemeral construct, perpetuating for an optimistic eternity this unrequited majesty: Barren existence is the thankless condition that is imposed where requirement and purpose are as irrelevant as a need to be aware that social relationships of any kind still carry the wishes of future encumbrance or familiarity in the face of this ephemeral transformation: Infinity is as patently imperceptible as the limitless presences that have their home in this airless redundancy where prayers and supplications are the whispers and songs of so many unrecounted memories, all clamouring with their silent voices, begging to be heard. The occasional social interactions, aside from the disturbing encumbrances that constantly litter this unlimited void with their interminable cries of regret and anger, are the sad songs that are most frequently superimposed with even sadder images that tell their own tales of optimism and anticipation to anyone who is prepared to listen, cast alone and adrift with the accommodating scent of a stultified gossamer in the clandestine current that still persists as the embodiment of all of the desires of spiritual attainment; the abiding essence of this magnanimous office.

6

The persistence of these vague indications continue to abound of where any fervent expectations of the perceived realities of this gigantic construct truly begin and where they truly end: The mysteries that are this conundrum of anticipation and confusion persist in the realms of the blessed and benign benefactors of this somnolent and eternal activity: True perceptions of vision and clarity however, are as rare and intangible as the opaque vistas that seem to me to be as elemental as the unrelentingly confused impressions that this beguiling antiquity continue to bequeath to me, imbibing experience with a dreadful sense of unutterable finality. This place is a chasm of the absolute; an infinity that imposes itself on this aching travesty with pleading prayers that cry out in adamant desperation for an eventual release and a tearful plea for solutions to all of the controversial conundrums that still linger as persistent supplications, all seeking for a direction that might yet provide them with all of the answers that they so desperately seek. Cultivated arrogance, the sore of repetitive past failings will, with the very best of new found intentions, continue to burnish this dedicated traveller with repeated assaults on his poor psyches' persistent memory residues: It would be presumptuous in the extreme of me to assume that I might enjoy any particular advantage pertaining to my own inhabitation of this place that might afford me an inflated impression of my own exclusivity: If that had been the case, I might then be able to employ those same subtle advantages to my own purpose in this isolated existence of essentially transcendental indifferences: In the desolation that is this omnipresent entirety that seems to have no end and no beginning either, the truths of the clamour that permeate this ether continue to be the soundless babble that persists as indistinguishable fabric breath in this universe and in the one that continues to rail at all of the sad intonations of contrition and regret, applauding all of the ailing promises that still persist as all of the emotional legacies.

7

These disgruntled memories still insist in insinuating this magnificent continuum with purposeful prayers that are the vestiges of all of the liberal intentions that still pertain as the fading litanies of so many lifetime promises and so many unrequited purposes: They have always existed as the bedrock of indifferent confidences and indifferent lies: The continuing need to justify these persistent elements of fading longings, the last remaining traces of which still linger as unrequited scores on which to play insidious tunes to uncertain faces, are the saddest elements of a lifetime that initially promised so much but which in the end seemed only to be its trailing architect, heralding the dawn of an unexpected new beginning.

8

The spiritual sensitivity of this place is entirely consistent with the normally accepted limits of socially acceptable intolerance, placating to some degree the omnipresent solitude that is distributed, or not as the case may be by the apparent hopelessness of so many of its permanently distracted souls: Perennial uncertainties are the measure that cannot be concealed if burgeoning guilt is to continue to be the noisome spectre that rears its ugly head to reveal itself to all who have any concerns as to its potency: The failings of these pasts are so deeply ingrained and so insidious as to persist as a canker in the mindset of these unfortunate beings: Insofar as they believe that they might yet discharge the awareness that still prevails, of those terrors, when they have finally dispensed their own final knowledge of their own previous existences: They might then succumb to the tentative realisation that their tribulations might yet be as persistent as the understanding of the reasons that caused that discomfiture to be so intense in the first place. Sadly, overall consciousness still remains the only realistic fabric of this place, decrying any of the needs for engaging with any of those anxious souls whose only hope of restitution lies in a more potentially successful future that might eventually prevail and mature for them; endowing them instead with a different and more doubtfully optimistic illusion that might eventually solidify with the sympathetic support of older transgression memories, allowing them all finally, the benevolent absolution of a timely benediction: As things remain however they will all continue to labour under the same unswerving conviction that they might one day be finally discharged from those same ancient sins, only to discover that they are still being burdened with those same previously disassociated memories instead.

9

Intuitive knowledge and awareness are the hand in glove of this place and the very fabric of its ephemeral atmosphere: They are the altercation of incessant regret and the implication of all of those other sorry circumstances that relate to the perpetuation of old songs and previous existences, whether by determined intent or simply due to the consequence of a dearth of sincere contrition: The engaging paradoxes that are the breath of this life and the anticipation of all of its rampant uncertainties all thrive here and are the relentless existences that maintain the promise of perpetual extenuation, even beyond any measurable degree of perception: Old associations carry the importance of historical significance to depend on, seeming not to favour the desires of need and want that have been the treasures feeding those traditional longings and the fruits of all of those so distant memory songs: The doubtful but ancient courtesies of privacy and secrecy have no place here but are instead the wail of all of those old memories that continue to play in whatever place it is that they still feel a need to be, in order to find any comfort; some small part of this integrated cosmic totality, sharing experiences that are the continuation of a lifetime that is the music of countless secrets; concealing the delicate trappings of untold whispered melancholies and joys. The importance and preservation of this past that was once of such relevance carries little of real purpose in the persistent requirement that pertains as unrequited alter existence adaptation, always legislating for differing needs and differing rules while we all attempt to coexist in this world of wholesomely congenial graces: Coexistence is intrinsically essential to the majesty of this limitless finality and any suspicion that one might still wish to pursue, relating to the denial of this perpetuation of unexpected circumstance only leads to disillusionment and disaffection in this most marvellous of infinities. The personal tragedies that do exist aggravate septic calm with avidly fondled latent bonds of memory that keep insisting that these inhibitive chains will still bind these souls, apparently irrevocably, to the final moments of previous lives that have never been satisfactorily severed by a recalcitrant past nor by any of the other disassociated memories either, that have never been thoroughly discharged as a consequence.

10

I seek, always with care for any new associations that might provide me with opportunities that I might ably employ, to interact with the recently arrived souls that occupy the spaces that I have taken care to enjoy as my own. It is reasonable to suppose that the recollections of distant and unrelated memories will eventually fade into a gloom of implausible might-have-been's, forever to be lost in the mists of this unpredictable adaptation that seems to me to exist primarily as promisingly sanctimonious retribution: As far as my own recollections of my own unsettled history are concerned I can only concur with the popularly accepted consensus of many of the other beleaguered exponents of this antiquated doctrine: Many of the souls who have been here before I arrived have also admitted to those same failures of memory when invited to reveal the significance of what should have been important memory moments in their own lives, that they might readily have been able to refer to with a similarly consummate ease.

11

So these doubts and misgivings all continue to pertain, a dimensionally superior quandary of misgiving and culpable restitution: I exist in this graveyard of questionable perspectives, so vast is it that its limitations remain as foreign and unobtainable to me as the unsettling majesty and the unlimited diversity that represents the unequivocally liberal habitation of this place and the interdimensional toast that is all of its secrets: I do find it difficult to interact with familiar acquaintances that I still remember from older and more different times, at a social level: I am unable even to achieve any kind of response by applying the most direct of songs: My aching prayers, whatever they might have meant to those errant recipients in their own pasts, seem not to be heard by them in this one: I can only assume that those same occupants that I knew from past lives are not even listening to me any more, not even in this one.

It would matter more to me if I was able to understand with certainty what my purpose is in this imposing solitude that I have been unable to comfortably cope with at this particular moment in time: My fertile imagination seeks constantly for answers to all the interminably pressing questions about the whole inscrutable scheme that is this overwhelmingly vast construct, but the music that greets my ears only responds with the annealing embrace of all of the other sympathetic souls that share those same signals of those same songs; small developments in the regeneration of their own restitutions; uniting eventually in a unified chorus of uncomfortably sanctimonious benevolence: I bask in the sincerity of their pleas and in the fervency of their contentions: The warmth is in their sensual vibrations, easing its tenuous strains throughout this glorified atmosphere that still persists as riotously rigorous grandeur: The comforting wisps of all of these generous indifferences remain as the careless embraces and the subliminal ecstasies that are its imperceptible melancholies, culminating finally in the persistent memory tunes that continue to encapsulate the fabric and the timbre of this divinely absolute infinity.

13

S usceptibly transparent future existences have always been available to all who have the ears and the inclination to perceive the inducements that are available to them all as benevolent succours, in the pursuit of their intrinsically transient and evasive perspectives, remaining always as their perceived goals in the attainment of their own spiritual end games: The gift that I still accept as being hermetically incorporated perpetuation in this universe is the one that most readily identifies with the needs and wants that are the raison d'etre of this infinite celebration. Comfort in this new eternity endears me to this continually congealing consciousness, so that the recollections that have been for so long the intrusive impediment of old but fading memories, now blesses me with an increasingly thorough understanding of everything that is important about this place and what it all really means to me, indicative of the demands and the restrictions that have been hermetically placed with me and with which I have been enabled to adapt and draw strength, despite my continuing efforts at discharging all of my previous yearnings and all of my previous limitations.

14

The novel extension of the new consciousness that I continue to interact with, seeks constantly for truths for me to sense and whisper at; imperceptible legislations and ominously discrete processes that seem determined to deny me the results of my own search, in spite of all of my best efforts to the contrary: At least that is how it seems to me to be in this intermediate term, so that I find myself perceiving all truth as though viewed through an indistinct and distorted window, blurred with continually vague perspectives that lack the generous integrity of the images that I so desperately desire to understand: Since it is all that seems to be available to me pursuant of this continuing quest of all of those disputed and unanswered questions, the images that I seek still insist on secreting themselves from the hunger of my needs in this secondary school that still maintains as rarefied spectral academy: Need is the fodder of a desire that cries out in its anguish and fills the very ether with the remonstrating pain of a persistent memory that haunts the imagination with the finality of its unrequited pleas for forgiveness: I discover for my toxic insecurity that the remnants of the retributions that constitute whatever errors there were that conspired to initiate the torments of those previous existences have not yet been readily discharged but have instead become the prevailing legacy of so many other untold future promises, persisting in the round as though the curses of desire and need had always been their previous home: Had that not been the case they might yet have been able to absolve those erstwhile impenitents from the pain of their ill gotten memories and from all of their related crimes, in the same breath that they have been elevated by newer restitutions that have been made available to them in this more amenable one.

15

The discomfort engendered by this rapidly emerging perception of new found visions has only served to highlight subliminally new awarenesses that seem to have increased exponentially in spite of the impending menace that exists as an emergingly latent anger: It has become as much a part of my obligation to seek for some parity in these disparate contradictions that prevent me from engaging amicably and whole heartedly with this new universe and also with its troubling karma, as it does my involvement with the magnificence that is all that I still perceive this hallowed place to be. The attainment of these new abilities has enabled me to cope more ably with the function of motion and the instance of travel; achievements that have improved considerably during this time, so that a simple wish or thought or even an expression of desire are now sufficient for me to arrive at any point that I want to be in, even though I might not even have been aware of that place that I had originally been seeking, to begin with: The distinction as always, lies in the discovery that when appreciations of ability do finally become part and parcel of acquired sangfroid acceptances of movement and achievement, I do find that, apart from intermittent rendezvous' that I occasion from time to time as a matter of course, there is actually little of real purpose that I wish to be involved with anyway, relating to this whole travelling exercise: With little of consequence or capability to inspire me relating to any of the uncounted spaces that exist as 'in betweens', it does mean that any ability to be in a particular place is simply one more indistinguishable variable since it remains the one place that I might once have wished to be in but does not of itself exist as a venue suitable for the interaction of mutually familiarising entities: In this place everywhere is everywhere and these 'everywheres' are the same as the ones that I have found to be everywhere else: Similarity is a perpetuating function in the persisting variation that exists between one place and time and any of the other places and any of the other times: The belief that a location might somehow be different in any way from any of the other ones is a concept that is as naïve as supposing that freedom to travel at all might somehow bequeath a traveller with a newer purpose and a newer vision: It might equally be concluded that the vagaries that persist in this realm relating to the need for a location or the lack of it, might reasonably be assumed to have limited viability in terms of any assumed reality at all Sadly there are none of these true perspectives of spacial equanimity here and no perceptible sense that is the available volume of all of these spaces either, that we might eventually be able to understand: There exists no palpable requirement for the maintenance of any of these pseudo physical impediments that it might have been necessary to apply, had the needs of those accommodations been anyway different: In the end, the abiding climate, whether it is found to be congenial or not, is the only worthwhile perception governing the aspects of all of the lives of all of the existences that still maintain as survival in this place.

16

The restitutions that are so involved with this iniquitous rebirth are the damning continuations of a deceptively ephemeral tranquillity: This new waking moment denies me knowledge of existences within any of the new realities that I am required to attain. The demands of this new genesis are a glaring sense that still pertains of my own insistence of a fuller understanding of these necessary perceptions and the engaging affinities that are this universe at its most magnificent and its most intricate: I bare all of my prayers, the better to perceive its awful grandeur and its persistent demand for the totality of my attention and the satisfaction of all that still remains of my emotional needs: I am comfortable with all of this in spite of my continuing complacency and my ignorance: I still feel that I have arrived at a philosophical fork in this oddly particular road that has always been cluttered with hypothetical nonconformities: Questions there are that continue to haunt me, particularly regarding the necessity and purpose of this apparently recalcitrant exercise: I still remain comfortable however with the understanding that a greater power than mine holds final sway as prime arbiter of all function and all purpose in this universal fantasy, enabling it just to fold itself over and return to its original condition of ultimate somnolence that was once its long sleep time, without ever needing to provide any of the answers that we have all been searching for, in the end: It does appear to me that these doubts and questions must have raised their complementary heads on many other occasions as well, more even than the lifetimes of all of the other entities who have arrived at this pass; longer even than mine.

17

Diversity is the unaccustomed grace that continues to preserve this limitlessness of permanent deliverance where there are no beginnings and apparently no diminishing finalities either. Perceptions plague every timbre of the consciousness that is this extraterrestrial habitat, promising only that the reality of the song might still play with me for as long as forever is able to torment me with truths that I might eventually discover the reality of, through the perpetuation of my own varied experiences: So I must continue to explore the value of these events and also of this particular outcome, whatever that might eventually reveal to me, in the persistent frugality that is this liberally exhilarating experience.

18

These recollections are all that still sustain me as perceptions that constitute my arrival in this existence with which I might at one time have been comfortable but which are now merely a recurring vision that continues to torment me: They are all the residues of the aging congealing harbingers of already fading memories that I continue to be uncomfortable with but which I still continue to remember as earlier existence moments; increasingly vague recollections of which I still continue to preserve for my endearing companionship and the diminishing awareness of a past life that has constituted the abrupt reversal of all of my remaining knowledge relating to pain and the discomfiture of errant memory, of which incidentally I am becoming increasingly less involved due to the impending diminution of all of those redundant histories and all of those old revelations relating to past lives that I now feel I no longer have either a need or a necessity for.

19

Arrival has been mostly akin to the blur that is the waking shock of this emerging vagrancy of paranormal confusion: Occurrence is the awareness that pursues these resistant acceptances of prior determination with such blessed somnolence and indifference that it continues to engage me with the beginnings of any new existence theory that I might previously have hoped to endear myself to as a salve for all of the hopes and all of the dreams that I might ever have held close to my heart, either in this life or in any of the previous ones, wherever or whatever they might have meant to me at the time that I first chose to engage with them.

20

W hile I am involved in absorbing the initial grains of uncertain truths that might enable me to comprehend the magnitude of all of these new experiences, it seems to me, in this period of newly discovered existence, that this poor soul might ultimately find itself mired in a condition of hopeless resignation and stultifying misdirection: I have been engaged with the consequences of this existential palindrome for what seems to me to have been an eternity, so that all that I have reasonably been able to do with it is to pursue these intentions with a headlong intensity that seems to me to be like the impulsive willingness of an impetuously misguided fool: I continue to assuage this tentative negativity with the cautious comfort of a possibly optimistic awareness that confident support, even from within myself might yet bring its own reward: Of that much I can be reasonably certain, but the palpitating disorientation that plagues these early attempts at assimilation and recognition that might have enabled me to identify more readily with the restrictions or the advantages that this new environment might have bequeathed to me, are the least of the lessons that I have yet to learn on this journey with which I am now so inextricably implicated.

I t does not serve me well to dwell on any of the events that might have led to, or indeed given me pause to question the reasons that have caused me to arrive in this place at all: They serve no purpose for me within the broader scheme of any of the discoveries that have persisted as dominant enigmas, the definitive complexion of which still remains this whole vast universe and the one with which I am now so thoroughly implicated: It is also the one with which I have now become more intrinsically involved as well.

22

The eloquence of these early messages about all of the possible finalities that might pertain, relating to existence and survival, have become much clearer to me: Much that had been important to me in my understanding of extraordinarily unfamiliar experiences into which I have so recently been introduced has now become more apparent to me: Even at this stage on my road of spiritual discovery, the properties that have governed all of these rules of engagement that have enabled coexistence to proceed in this new lifetime are, of necessity privy to this unique eternity into which I have recently been introduced. It is not too difficult to appreciate that many of the emotional frailties that I have come to depend on in this lifetime of recent memory are not actually the inclement truths that bear any real relevance for me. It is not difficult also to appreciate that many of the conditions that I have come to depend are not actually relevant to this space or time any more: The concept that had always been understood as being an essential ingredient in the servicing of 'time' has itself become a pointlessly irrelevant mental chattel in the convoluted perception that still controls this habitually exclusive environment: With the vocal propensity that is this uninhibited profusion of diverse entities, all of which share this same universe that I myself have become such an integral part of, I now realise that the importance of coexistence with my fellow beings, whatever that might actually have involved, is a necessary precursor to understanding what is actually required of me in terms of learning how best to interact with all of the needs and all of the requirements that exist at this level.

23

The concept of 'time' has evolved of its own accord into a marked degree of irrelevancy in the function of the sensual forces that have always been in play and with which an innate understanding of existence is the only really determining parameter: It contains no perceivable reference for any essential regulation governing the requirement that is this rampant extension of apparent perpetuity within this place: Moments continue to fade into a blissful infinity with the imperceptible insignificance of so many of the normal motions, needs and the continuing importance of 'whens' and 'hows' that have always helped them to prevail in their pasts as well. The relevance of servitude, when concerned with the diligence and attention that has always been paid to the subservience of time, has always been related to stricter disciplines than mine, imposed as conditions to be preserved when they are applied to other universes that have different physical needs and consequently more unsympathetic survival criteria as well. As it is, since none of these particular restrictions serve any real purpose in the perpetuation or otherwise of this particular existence, the importance that is demanded of it is simply the redundant regulation of an apparently obsolete concept that serves no requirement or function for its continuation in this one. Life will always maintain as a momentary perspective with none of the impedimenta that has been generated by need or want, the avid pursuit of which will always persist as the manna of the unobtainable.

24

The importance that has always been eagerly endorsed in the past, of maintaining existence at a material level, is one that I am now finding myself increasingly distracted by. Memories still maintain of a lifetime that is now an irrelevance in the dedicated pursuit of the more salient factors of newly acquired endeavours: Older, relentlessly restrictive attachments still direct me toward what seem at first glance to be the natural expressions of a rationale, still continuing to impose a restrictive value on me: In spite of these irrelevances and the persistent stipulations of these erstwhile existences, they actually bear no comparison to the older applications that belong in a past life or even to the one that I am living in now.

25

The enchantment that is this new circumstance of splendid tranquility seems, in varying degrees to radiate its more beneficial influences throughout all of the spectral parameters that appear to me as limitlessness in an existence that I am becoming increasingly comfortable with. A nervous suspicion is, however beginning to intrude on my rarefied susceptibilities to the extent that I am becoming increasingly more reflective of imperceptible understandings that linger as the latent parameters of other mischievous associations, alerting me to the awakening conviction that all might not be the ideally comfortable melange of lucid atmosphere and integrated substance that I had initially become accustomed to: This new life has engendered the most discreet of discomfitures, concealing itself within a communal cordiality that has always been the object that was at its heart and is the raison d'etre of all of these amicable associations, with all of the persistent ambiguities that still maintain as the essences of this spiritual community: The perception persistently prevails that true understanding is essential in maintaining a condition of 'self' and is the requirement that has become most intimately involved, with an increasing relevance to the development of this expanding consciousness and its subsequent satisfactory fulfilment: This glorious exposition has become the vindication of all of my hopes and all of my ambitions relating to an ever increasing involvement in this so clandestine metamorphosis: I still continue to believe that real achievement might just be a stone's throw away from all of the new discoveries that could be so metaphysically better for me in the longer term: I think that I might even have it within myself to improve at a broader level than anything that I might previously had hoped to have achieved hitherto; or even that I might possibly accomplish in any of the 'afterwards' that I still continue to hold out for as possible futures: It is even conceivable that I might even be able to comprehend this fabric of regenerated conformity into which I have been integrated so that it might even enable me to expand my own levels of awareness even further, of all of the previously tenuous and exclusive aspects that have constituted all of my past existences: A promise that has consistently eluded me hitherto and which has continued to operate against me as a potential barrier, limiting any real understanding of the reasons for these existence premises that actually govern the regulation of this place in its entirety: In this intermediate environment and its unfolding universe that I have eagerly embraced and which now so completely dominates my existence needs and my spiritual integration, I do realise that acceptance of this new reality, based on all of the available insights will not permit me to embrace this collective and unlimited entirety and absorb, with full understanding, its subliminal messages, the culmination of all of my recent achievements and all of the spiritual delicacies to which this existence has so generously contributed.

26

I enjoy an enhanced degree of perception in relation to the requirements of this place with the purposeful acquiescence of a liberal tranquility that allows me to view the direction that I am required to take to discover the breadth and the cornerstone that relates to this new wisdom: It has allowed these adjustments and adaptations to improve my well-being in ways that have enabled me to more comfortably reap the rewards that have permitted me to become more adapted to prospects relating to any potential new destiny and to more effectively follow the direction of a possible purpose, in whatever form that might ultimately reveal itself to me to be. Due to the reversal of so many of those recently spiritual impediments and to all of those other erstwhile encumbrances, I am now arriving at a point in this new life when I might reasonably suppose that I will finally be able to dispense with all of the emotional trappings that have involved me in so many of the initial setbacks to the attainment of all of my ambitions and to all of my initial hopes and dreams: What pleasures there are that might still be gained when I no longer need to be distracted by outdated emotional foibles that only make the higher demands of this existence more difficult to grasp and even harder to achieve.

27

The encumbrance of this melange of apparently directionless spiritual disturbance only serves to increase any doubts that I might still have nurtured during this time: The infusion of diversely emotional responses and debilitating confusions are the perpetuating chorus of countless souls railing to their own Gods for an absolution and for some guidance, with the questionable assistance of a more positive social direction: Their passionate convictions continue to insist that they might still be able to engage more comfortably with the needs of a cultural obscurity with which they are no longer currently involved, permitting them to take on a more active role in the other activities that might enable them to interact more fully with their fellows than they have been able to do in their own recent pasts: The anger and the resentment that they still persist with and feed off from, one to the other, are the pathetic travesties of a regret and an admonishment that still prevails as painful and harrowing legacy, particularly when it is engaged with their own attempts at punitive interaction: I continue to maintain my own efforts, keeping as clear of these disturbing influences as it is possible for me to do: We all exist as a single unified entity, the consequence of so many integrated lifetimes that have involved us all in maintaining our own degrees of integrity as part of the same gigantic, complete and intangible whole: I do try, with a visible determination to involve myself with the newer and less assured generations that have also recently arrived here, only to discover that those same trappings and those same retributions still persist, and have always lived here with them in their own pasts, with the same relationships relating to them that I have discovered, relating to myself in those same moments when I first arrived.

28

The needs of engagement and involvement with the unsettled masses that reside here in vast and uncounted numbers have developed into an art that I have rapidly learned to deal with, due to my own earlier interventions into this benevolently madcap experience: It is reasonable to suppose that I have actually become more accustomed to these unlikely circumstances and have become even more adapted to this arbitrary co-existence that I continue to share with all of my contemporaries: I feel consistently more secure about avoiding the tears and the acrimony that are all of the lives that have become the embodiment of singularly personal tragedies, pursuing me into all of the more secret places in which I have always been able to avail myself of the replenishing illusion of a blessed emotional release and a more benevolent succour. The anguished scores of all of these souls, with their rage and their complaints, remain as painful artifacts to me now, emotional intolerances that vagrant circumstances have forced me to become more accustomed to and even occasionally to tolerate with a recalcitrant plausibility: This continuing and unabating cacophony persists without pause as an infectious effusion of frustrated energy and unrequited emotion: Awful desperation is the rail of countless tearful prayers, carried out by unified voices; attempting to applaud the remonstrations of pain, regret and melancholy that are the insidious endowment of remotely related discomforts, together with their continually tremulous repentances: I pray constantly that they might still find a moment in their own good time that might yet enable them to be free of the limitations that have been imposed on them by the implications of their own life paths, with the same degree of restitution that might then enable them to finally obtain a more positive acknowledgement of themselves and their own existences than has been so unsustainable for them up to this point in their own pasts.

29

The wails of petulant acrimony spread their seed far beyond the perceived limitations of this sanctified veil of tears: The intrusions into these deselected spaces remain as dark moments to me, involving me in some accidental incursions that have devolved themselves into rarified expressions of violence and intimidation, leaving me implicated in the most awful expressions of incomprehensible aggression and mindless rage: It is true that I take the greatest of care to avoid the places where these dark energies are known to feed: The strands that bind the elements that opt to exist in these planes, to other places that they insist on claiming as their own, enables them to sustain their own vibrant but cohesive energy; a consequence of latently empathic bonds of a mutually exclusive animosity that is then directed towards the unfortunate souls that have been reckless enough to venture into these deselected places at all: Previous existences can hardly have been a sufficient reason that might be easily explained, for the obsessions that have endorsed these prohibitive preserves, and the impact that they still have today, when those same memories and materials are engaged to carry that same emotional content; the meat of all of those matters for them, into those same sad moments again: The awful power that is this misguided energy will always carry dangers of its own when it is engaged for purposes other than those for which it was never actually meant to be applied: Mental contradictions, many driven by an enduring antipathy and powered by unbridled bitterness, do insist that any voluntary ostracism, if only for the purposes of one's own personal safety, are the only reasonable conclusion that might be drawn on, when involving oneself with unpleasant confrontations, face to face.

30

The direction of this malicious energy is both diverse and varied, expressing itself as an abnormally undesirable and subliminally vindictive suggestion, bound around with the indelible strands of a deviously persistent benevolence: The power of this uncontrolled rage can and does extend itself into all of the other realms as intrusive interference; places where they would not normally have had any right or reason to be: These conditions even extend, on occasion, into the different places and different times that can and do disturb the accepted and established status quo that has always existed in the past, for the purposes of non-intervention into other understood and undefined customary parameters: They continue to exist as force in these places and comfortably relate to all of the other undisturbed and undernourished alternative spaces that still exist in those various other planes of existence as well: It is entirely probable that these entities, when they do choose their moment to intervene in any of the other related schemes of things, intend only on encroaching into places and times with which they might once have been comfortable, but which they now persist with, only as the prevailing substances of old but irrelevant memory songs, intent only on imposing their mischief or discomfort on those unfortunate present day incumbents: They continue to be empowered, either willingly or unwillingly to intervene in the conduct of matters pertaining to these places, not so much because of a need to be alive to the consequences of their actions, as it is to the continuing promise of the perpetuation of their present day agonies and comforts that continue to persist as present day needs: They might then continue to draw on the indelible continuation of those unfortunate past experiences and in the residues of those past lives, in the one that they are continuing to live in today.

Of concern to me as I continue to dwell on this particular issue is the persistent dilemma relating to my own spiritual condition: It would be naïve and arrogant of me after all to suppose that I exist simply as an individual entity in this place, blessed with all of the assumed perception of privileged exclusivity: With the vast numbers that live together here, such assumptions carry as little of credibility as the exaggerated misconceptions of a miscreant day dreamer who insists in believing that this world is his to do with as he pleases: My own defining moment will surely arrive, as it must for every soul that has ever had the good fortune to pass through this place, gifted with the same realisations of whatever it was that all of this ever really meant to them: When the mists of memory do finally part for me, I might actually recover the comforting perception that will stay with me as that final gift, of one last look at all of these deviously sinuous threads of subtly miscreant interference and all of these benevolently insidious deceptions that still continue to haunt me, scattering the concepts of all the value that those exquisitely flavoured qualities ever really meant to me, into one last fading groan of understanding and regret.

32

For the time being, I can only continue to tread this mystical path with a provincial delicacy, proceeding on my own culturally articulated journey with the blasé expectation of a continually fortunate involvement in this oddly occasional space and time: My own perceptions of myself and my environment are all of the things that I have ever desired them to be or perhaps what it has actually pleased me for them to be, notwithstanding the revisited personality with which I am now comfortably endeared: I still think of myself occasionally in an old personal way, perhaps with the sadness of a redundant desire that I still preserve from some of the cherished identity that still maintains as wistful memory chocolate, flavouring these old but original familiarities with a lingering fondness: I do cherish the reality of this spiritual conditioning and the limitations and capabilities that have since been conferred on me in the name of the person that I might once have wished to become: Clearly there are some new changes to these circumstances that I am adapting more readily to and with which I have been more able to bask in this cradle of the most benign of contents. I move with an ease now, (motion is desire) with a 'want' as sufficient as 'need', to rare places in which I might comfortably share a thought, experience and interaction with others who have the same care and the same consideration: Still and all, I do spend a lot of my time alone, with my own thoughts and my own misgivings concerning my own personal circumstances and the questionable tenure of this oh so exhilarating consciousness: With a mild desperation I still treasure a longing that persists as the remnant of a history that has enabled this perpetuation of so many distant pasts, tending them with an uncertain trepidation, reminiscent of a recalcitrant child holding onto what still remains of his most treasured keepsakes: Stubborn determination binds me inexorably to these past existences and might still shield whatever it is that is still left of my prevailing sanity from these insidiously rare recollections, knowing also that I still have little ultimate control over the intrusive functions that define all of my future anticipations and all of my future prosperity as well.

33

I am unsure about whether these continually conflicting questions are just the spice of congenital inhibitions that continue to colour all the old impressions that have been my standby and my friend: The breaths of this newly sanctified experience have begun slowly and insidiously to squeeze all of the free-flavoured assumptions that have been so preciously preserved by me up to this time, casting them finally into a deliberately sentimental pool of reluctantly discarded optimistic keepsakes: I do appreciate the importance of conviction and purpose in a world that maintains on the strength of dubious doubts and dubious definitions but I do have to question with some temerity the persistent requirement of this misleading insanity that refuses even to respond with answers to the questions that I have persistently pursued, if only due to the inherent and prolonged forbearance that permits me to better understand the reasons for this subliminally divisive degradation.

34

I remember, barely, many of the events and actions that have been part and parcel of my earlier life and also of my earlier survival condition that I have not yet been able to adequately relate to, compared with any of the ones that I have since experienced in this newer life, with all of the unpredictable uncertainty about the strength of its reliability and of the same perceived inaccuracies that have since become available to me: The importance of these recollections of past times are not as obvious to me as I had hoped that they might have been: It would be naïve of me to suppose that had I lived the sort of life that had been devoid of error and interaction, I might not now be so confronted with newer and more impinging regrets of my own: I hear and feel a longing that comes from the desperate concern that redemption and absolution might not actually be the balm that will provide those ultimate blessings of repentance and salvation, in any way that it might be possible for me to attain them: For myself, the failings and devastations over which I no longer have any control and perhaps no hope of restitution either, remain with me in this place, continuing to torment me as well: Sorrows cry out with their strains of remorse and regret, so loudly do they call in the din that is the very timbre of this dreadful anxiety and longing, the wailings of unforgiveness that, even in the midst of this impenetrable cacophony, constitute so much of the need for the beguiling comfort of sympathetic remedies: It is my continuing desire for a similar identity than that with which I might yet be able more readily to relate, in terms of a permanently mutual attraction and a similarity that will sit more comfortably with this sympathetic emotion ethos: I might then be more able to identify with those same stipulations that might eventually anneal the recollections of all of those old pains and all of those old regrets that constantly intrude on every thoughtful moment of this tortured fabric and cause me such persistent discomfort.

35

The driving force in this place continues to be the perseverance of emotional resilience: It is the defensive mechanism with which we have all become encumbered and which only serves to provide us with all of the mechanisms for our own protection and for our own security: The existence of these invasive emotional impediments continue to work their insidious craft into the negative constraints that are always those same expressions of fear and anger: And how they do feed and fawn at all of our doubts and all of our desperations; the grist of this oh so disparate mass of hopeless life that keeps asking only that they might be permitted to comprehend the answers to the questions that might finally allow them some comfort and some solace as well: There is the dark too! The pervasive and insidiously negative kind, born of a gloom of rampant malignancy and brooding hatred: I regard it all with every cautious perception of my conscious being as it continues to feed off the doubts and the suspicions of reneged and misguided identities, spreading their sinuous fronds with intimations of anger and melancholy, attempting ever to interpose malevolence and hatred into all of those seemingly vacuous spaces that comfort only dark images and even darker songs. The music is always the same though and the transparency of the invasive messages always readily apparent, particularly to the newer and less acquainted travelers, as the respective needs of their uncertain futures have been able to make it for them.

36

Past histories are the detritus of increasingly distant memories with only emotional links still lingering, to enable them to finally move on: This recalcitrant gel continues, with obstinate indifference to bind my soul to the listless remnants of a redundant melancholy that lingers in my mind as the score of all of the old tales and those even older social impediments: The distractions of any of these previous times, with the encumbrances of their associated memory burdens, still sit as unwanted emotional legacy and then only as insignificant attachments of them, at least in the remaining fullness of their more defining moments.

37

Past personal histories have none of the relevance to present day circumstance with which I have grown so accustomed and with which I now comfortably coexist: The tedium that involves this constant obeisance to the maintenance of all that this old physical shell ever really meant to me was that it has always remained the one thing that I was once so concerned to attend to and care for, for such a long and unqualified time: Now this unbounded liberty is a newly discovered freedom, enabling me to interact and engage with at will and to enjoy as a new and unrestricted mobility for the rest of the time that is left to me to employ in this place.

38

I t might best be described as one of those oddly inspiring waking moments that reveaed itself to me occasionally in the midst of all of the other vaguely incidental perceptions that still persist as a flavoured transition between subtly incoherent quasi existences and a newer and entirely more irrelevent expectation that is in itself a newer experience conundrum: I find that it constitutes the metaphysical panacea of a spiritual perfection, the truly formative freewheeling variety that I am experiencing now, not so much because I seem finally to have woken to a new awareness of the differences in my own personal conditioning, as it is to the fact that they are no longer related to any of the associated impediments that I have always been implicated with from any of my past lives, and the new day attendances that have since been retrospectively related to them in this one as well: The principal functions that involve the mechanics of motion no longer carry any relevance for me in this place where conditions that can only be described as superbly special, allow me free movement in any direction and to any place in which I wish to be.

39

U nderstandings of the principles of time are, of themselves perceptions that are fading into the mists of a mind numbing perpetuity in this obscure world of random oblivions with which I am now thoroughly engaged, continuing to be permitted the liberty of frequently misguided expectations for my sins: In the belief that I might yet be allowed some relief from the frantic misdirection that continues to promise me secrets, I can only drift aimlessly in the pursuit of vaguely existential paradox's that might actually be the separations of illucid differences of perception that I might more comfortably be able to relate to in terms of any of the previous moments that I might once have existed in: Unable to refer this present one to any of those erstwhile predetermined parameters and certainly not to any of the ones that are even remotely physical in this ultra-spiritual establishment, I wait in tentative expectation for that implausible moment when all of my hesitations and all of my misgivings will be translated into an explosion of unadulterated appreciation and understanding.

40

Loneliness is such a transient perception in the paranormal travesty that constitutes this residue of broken promises and even more broken dreams. They are all here, in this place that has no name and no representation of any kind that might ably relate it to what has always been popularly perceived reality either: Deep emptiness and regret are the recurring pains of loss and recrimination, crying out through the wastes that are this ethereal soup of misaligned alter-spirituality, pleading with unified voices for answers that might yet assuage the need for a recognition of purpose or indeed of some other residual absolution of past failures and errors that might ever have constituted those ailing existences in previous times.

41

Past lives are but the glimmer of sensations and smiles that continue to feed off the desperate need to retain some vestige of an existence that only harbours a knowledge of darker moments that have constituted those failing memories and the subsequent desire for an absolution: I would share some of that comfort with you if I could, recalling those moments of my own that have been the reference points of my own early recollections of this place; then perhaps I might more ably relate them to my own more diverse memory moments as well and better establish a more reasonable explanation of my own persistent doubts and my own personal dilemmas.

42

This melange of acrimony and joy are the grist of the why's and the wherefores that persist as the tenuously tactile soup of this universe; as absolute as any limited perception can allow it to be: It is the ultimate harvest of all that was ever perceived of as being the promise of a benediction that might finally dispense with all of the disputations and all of the doubts that have enabled conflict and contradiction to grow and fester even within the spiritual bounds of this existential tabernacle: Beside the reflected emotions that uncounted many's have claimed as their own are the external tribulations of regret at the failings of all of those pasts when they continued to cultivate those racking tears, persisting as the bane of all of those disenchanted souls: Their wailing cries of contrition might yet be their saviour and the blessing of eternal absolution might better enable them to finally achieve the ultimate release that they so desperately desire: So the damage of persistent scars lingers as the malignant wounds of a tireless ignominy, discharged eventually to the four winds of a spiritual discreditation, commensurate with the fullness of this persistently imperceptible occasion: So many of them there are here, in this place, desolate and lost, seeking only for a direction and a purpose that might yet apply to them the indelible balms of tranquility and succour, alleviating to an indeterminate degree, the weight of a guilt that continues to fester in their memories and in their songs, seeming never to fade, even in the final years that have constituted so much of the pain that remains even now, in their tears and in their tragedies.

43

The evidence of this emotional duress resides here both in the abundance of its perpetuation and in the power of its various rancid regrets as well: So wildly and frantically does it feed with the eager desperation of so many unfulfilled requirements and so many unsatisfied needs: Memories are the tales that tell of loss and disappointment, drifting in this turbulently cosmic waste with the unbridled tension of an angry raging storm, beating at the sensitivities of this misdirected mass of weeping waste, pleading only for some vestige of a creative absolution to avail themselves of, that might yet pacify the turbulence that has been all of these unrequited suppositions: Their cries of anguish batter at my disjointed perceptions as I ease my way through this relentless cacophony of universal desolation in silent and determined reflection: Still they insist, those ever present cries of undulating pain and sorrow, more tangible even than the pains that are its eternal travesties, persisting as unrequited lives themselves in the wake of their frantic desperation: Their anger continues to feed off countless false forgivenesses that lie in waiting entrapment for the beguiling deception of supposedly purposeful renewal; the stored and preserved residues of all of those past lives that are the strengths, sufficient to the prevailing moment and to the venom that still continues to persist in perpetuating itself as violent emotional impediment: Sadly the subsequent responses are invariably reflected in those same new found moments of anger and hatred as well.

44

I am uncomfortable with the realisation of these unexpected conditions and circumstances that insist on the governance of a related intellect and ambience: I have arrived at a point of acceptance in the adoption of this rare necessity with all of its inevitable interactions. I do share the dilemma that these questions have raised with the many occupants that have also lived here, all with their similar circumstances of congenial harmony and interaction and many with whom I am now quite familiar. They have all contrived to become more universally amicable assists with the concerted effort of other similarly well intentioned acquaintances that I have been able to relate to in the time that I have spent here, that with the unified effort of us all, we have been able to distract or avoid these consistent threats of belligerency: I do not doubt that when the day does finally arrive that my time in this place does come to its end, that those who still remain here will probably have to deal with similarly intimidating complications in much the same way that I have had to do, as well.

45

I do realise that the circumstances that have intruded into my thought processes with these unwelcome feelings and visions are also beginning to impose their own subtle altercations on some of the mildly intrusive perceptions that I have discovered within myself and over which I seem to have no direct control and which indeed I am even at a loss to fully understand the reason for: The prevailing conditions or even many of the conceivable outcomes of them, all appear likely to involve me in significant changes of one kind or another, to this present life condition: In what form and to what purpose these changes might apply, I am still uncertain of what that outcome might be at this particular point in time: I seek constantly for similarities that I have always been able to draw on for my own comfort and for my own assurances, sensing only that there is now rather less of the raucous retribution that has always played such a significant role in this life but which has lately been substituted for with different and more subtle altercations of atmosphere and timbre that have become an altogether more sensitively benign form of experience.

46

Selective consciousness is not likely to serve me in the same way that I have been comfortable with in my recent past but neither is the threat and discomfiture that has prevailed on me in my search for suitably amicable conditions of peace and calmness, always threatening, in spite of my best measures at avoidance, to rear its head yet again, even in the name of the new life discoveries that I am entertaining now.

47

Tentative examinations of this place reveal nothing to me that bears any kind of familiarity with any of the places that can I recall having been in hitherto: All that I am certain of is that this new and novel appraisal of my present life condition bears no relation to any of the ones that I have been engaged with in any of my recent pasts but appears instead to offer a unique and oddly alien proposition to me: These rare sensations still hold a defining depth of purpose in terms of all of the new promises that this period of variable circumstances might still involve me in: Physical activity per se, seems hardly to be the essential prerequisite of this uniquely new survival condition so that I remain content to bask in the strangely restrictive confinement that is this tranquil balm of mildly insipid liquidity.

48

The overriding sensation of these unfamiliar surroundings is the annealing presence of alternative controlling intelligences and the certainty that my own safety in this new environment has already been established within the cosseting limitations that are the promise of some newer world order: Variations of this uncertainty condition, which appear now to have become my new reality, remain as a consistently newer familiarity association and incorporate the amusing comfort of sympathetically caring songs, still feeding this semi-combative awareness with subtly extraneous but jocularly positive messages: I bask in the cautious detriment that is all of these mysteriously tenuous influences and all of these similarly related vocal distractions that all continue to persist as the more dubious involvements of this controversial intolerance.

49

The glimmer of latent recollections teases this umbilical yearning for lost spaces and lost times: It seems just a short while ago that positive engagements with sympathetic minds had become so completely a way of life for me that I had comfortably adjusted to the promises of that existence and had actually become sufficiently ingratiated with it all that I had found myself struggling to recall any of my earlier reference moments when life conditions had been an altogether separate proposition.

50

I am suspended in the fluid expanse of a strangely intrinsic sensitivity, attempting constantly to suppress the more unsettling of vagrant premises that might indicate that it was heralding the beginnings of a new and more amenable era in this continuing regeneration lifestyle, with an irrepressible trepidation: I seek constantly for any confirmation that these deceptively tactile comforts and crystal clear revelations of which I have now become more acutely aware, are truly the new circumstance that I am still so nervously conscious of, but which I still fear might only be the disturbing remnant of some old surviving social contradiction that remains as the harbinger of an acrimony and self-doubt that still persists as vague memory association that I am determined not to trust absolutely, concerned only that I might begin to believe absolutely in this irrepressible renaissance that has returned once more to reappoint this newer reality and replenish the thesis which has been all my other previous memory moments.

51

Time passes slowly in this intemperate void of moist immobility: I have now arrived at an understanding of the circumstance that I have so recently been introduced to; much of it plainly physical restriction that I am required to tolerate for the determining necessity of my basic comfort needs and my emotional contentment as well: It is all that remains of me in this disturbingly literal perception of new life conditioning; the perpetually indeterminate association that still maintains as an integral part of some new lifetime promise that has been forcibly implicated within this perennially inactive wealth of vacuous liquidity: I hear, taste and feel all of the life that surrounds me; no stranger now, to the tentative admission of my own cautious concerns and my own security: Uncertainty still lives with me in the remnants of a dubious satisfaction culture, persisting as its most abiding feature and the ultimate determination that has always been the care and the cultivation of my own personal well-being: The volume and the activity of this autistic benevolence, directed always towards the servicing of my own quasi physical selfishness, remains unrestricted by any of the newer stranger awarenesses and the newer stranger sensitivities that have been all of the related applications of unique and customary liabilities, achieving their deliberate movement within the limits of this uniquely improbable confinement.

52

My understanding and my awareness of these new primitives are the palliatives of a newly discovered emotion and might even become memorable keepsakes in this persistent panoply of unanswered questions: The delicacies of care and contact, whether by sound or by the gentlest of touches, are the essences of all that I might ever have dreamed of attaining through the effort of my own so avaricious needs: For now, all that I am permitted to do is to engage with this new revelatory circumstance and attend to the realities of a brave new world that consists of new sounds and even newer activities, drinking my fill of this overflowing cup of emotional sensitivity and banking all of my rampant imagination in this merciful exercise that is all that still maintains of this implausibly physical integration.

53

Constant activity torments my sensibilities so that I am no longer able to fully appreciate the implications of any of the loudly excessive altercations that continue to affect my personal disposition and my individual well-being: The persistent battering that has been the consequence of so many irregular constrictions causes me much physical discomfort and is the benevolence of a consistently violent attrition over which I no longer have any control: The variegated sounds, with other increasingly persistent regularity that I have found to be so painful, are the irregular tears of unconditional misery and undisguised apathy, generated as expressions of an adversely resigned emotional content: I wonder how much of this interference is actually due to my own personal involvement in protracted issues relating to this new lifetime litany with which I have become so intrinsically implicated.

54

I am uncertain about the conditions under which this diverse range of peculiar circumstances continues to maintain: It seems such a long time ago now that the discomfort that I first felt began for me: I do appreciate the significance of a condition that continues to be as contradictory for me as the physical dissimilarity that is all of the other anciently misleading pleasure moments: I still regularly associate myself with older memories that linger, even in this present, as persistently familiar and amiable associations, waiting only to irritate me as habitually unwelcome futuristic handicaps; they persist now only as ancient memory residue: The resulting pain and the subsequent fear gifts that have steadily evolved due to this strange new experience culture, is consistent with a dearth of many of the usual memory traces that are frequently related associations and a persistent lack of any understanding of the reasons for any of these new emotional strictures, incumbent with my present predicament but also due to the imposition of present day circumstances: I know little now of consequence of any of the comforting palliatives that I have relied on for so long for my emotional sustenance, still persisting only as the abiding sanctity of a relentlessly jaundiced past.

55

The pain! The pain! Dragging, pleading, begging pleading; so humbling and so invasive: I so hurt! The squeeze and the pain: The screams and the pleas are the petulant anxieties that jar at all of my raging sensitivities: This torture seems not to have an end, contesting all of my conjugal rights to the validity of this indeterminate resuscitation and the persistent denial of all of my comforts in this space that I have come to love as my home and my sacristy: Desperation engages the determination that I should never be removed from this place, even for the doubtful satisfaction and security of all of the other worlds of which I know too little to be adequately confident about ever having been even a small part of: All of my prevailing doubts and all of my assailing uncertainties continue to compound as I pursue the determination of all of my fondly encapsulated past existences, in this one.

56

Do your worst, you barbarous bullies! I will not be removed from my tenuously secure seclusion; my claim and my comfort for so long that I am certain enough of all of my time in here to remain secure within it: I am more likely to regard it as the more abiding of certainties than any of the future prospects confronting me of newer worlds and newer habitats, with a singular degree of relative indifference.

57

Oh shock! Finally, reluctantly I relinquish this defining security that has been such an amenable and delicate prison: An amicably ordered comfort universe for what appears to me instead to be the alternative promise of an uncertain lifetime and an even more uncertain existence: I continue to tolerate these physical intrusions for the indeterminate duration of this tenaciously pleasurable final conflict that has been for so long part of a fluid world, the same one that has been my home and my comfort for what has been such an immeasurably long time: Already I perceive new dangers that herald the beginnings of newer and more faltering memory moments: The fright gasp of this new attrition is the bitter wisp of the colder air, so heavy is it with the sounds that are so much cause in this emotional attrition: Light glazes my sight: Bright light!; so bravely does it burn, yet so angrily: A shock! A scream!: They are all the sounds and the smells that persist as threats of denial of all of the promises that ever existed for me as home of future comfort, all of which I had anticipated with a mild sensibility: Now the only song that I hear is the one that sings of future dangers and of a newer and more deliberate alienation: It is the same fear song that promises always to stay with me, even though it is still the same as the one that has been of my own making and is also of the making of so many others as well: I do fear this new cold and all of the other associated tensions and all of the other danger songs that I still hear so well: Strength is in the light, warning only of danger and of an injudicious insecurity: Comfort, be my friend!

Warmth and comfort, rare joys that I know so little of, yet still so much need for want of love and all of the pain that is waiting for me in the light and in all of the sweet attention: Caring hands and caring comforts.

Now at last I see you all! With your smiles and your acceptances, I see you!: Light is still my pain but I do see you through it all: I know you all as well from all of those other times that have been the same as the one that I return to once again, disrupting all of these old flavoured perceptions, playing the same insidious tunes for me again one more time: Trepidation is mixing with all of the trust and all of the doubt of who I really am or even of who I once might have been: Trust is in all of who I can be; let that remain my continuing legacy All that remains for me now is to close these eyes one final time and hope, with all of my heart that when they are opened again, my future will have been amicably rearranged: Whether that arrangement will be for the better or for the worst still remains to be discovered.

✦ ✦ ✦ ✦ ✦

I see your watered eyes through watered eyes:
Tears are pleasures smiles: Tears and surprise
Wallow in my nakedness and my despair:
Fawning gasps for breath in this inclement air.

Are promise and regret the only friends I feel:
Mesmerized awaking chitter chatter pleas:
Hands that hold, embrace these tender childhood fears:
Grasping loving eyes, so deep, so clear.

ABOUT THE AUTHOR

The author was raised within the confines of a religious order of nuns called THE POOR SISTERS OF NAZARETH from his earliest age until he was discharged into the real world at the tender age of fifteen years. He was placed into their care from the age of two weeks and spent the entirety of his childhood under their supervision.

His continuing development continued to be an abiding stricture since the necessary guidance of life experience and education were not the life supporting criteria that ever figured heavily in any life time preparations, as far as the nuns at Nazareth House were ever concerned.

He has always been an avid reader, even from the earliest age and has always enjoyed an engaging affinity with all of the aspects and all of the uses of his language.

He is particularly fond of the writings of Shakespeare and has always been intrigued by the writers intricate literary artistry and by his linguistic perceptions.

He is a lover of most forms of poetry but struggles with the more modern genres that fail to engage with any of what are considered to be popularly accepted patterns or structures, or even the occasional but liberal employment of the odd capital letter.

The patterns of his life have been very much a transient affair with constant variations in his search for a purpose being constantly the driving force that has led him to seek for more varied or challenging lifetime opportunities as he progressed his way through it.

He has always maintained an abiding passion for all aspects of aviation and he considers himself fortunate to have lived during a time when these pleasures and excitements were still available for him to experience and enjoy.

He has already published two books: "POETIC RAMBLINGS OF A DISENCHANTED SOUL" and "A NAZZY HOUSE BOY" that have been printed and distributed, one of which is a collection of his poems and the other that tells the story of his own early upbringing.

He considers himself blessed to have had four fine grandchildren to his name to whom he is entirely devoted.

He thanks God for all of his blessings and all of the opportunities that have come his way during a longish and varied life: Who knows what the rest of it will bring to him in his future.

Printed in Great Britain
by Amazon